About
Skill Builders
Introduction to
Music

by Kaylynne Fox

Welcome to Rainbow Bridge Publishing's Skill Builders series. Like our Summer Bridge Activities™ collection, the Skill Builders series is designed to make learning both fun and rewarding.

Skill Builders Introduction to Music makes basic principles of music easy and understandable for young children and beginners. Exercises and activities help teach musical beats, high sounds and low sounds, rhythm, musical patterns, dynamics, notes, the musical staff, instrument families, and more. Pages include book work, hands-on tasks, and "get-up-and-move" activities to help reinforce concepts for multiple learning styles.

Activities to encourage your child's creativity and higher-level thinking skills are also included.

Learning is more effective when approached with an element of fun and enthusiasm—just as most children approach life. That's why the Skill Builders combine entertaining and academically sound exercises with eye-catching graphics and fun themes—to make reviewing basic skills at school or home fun and effective, for both you and your budding scholars.

D1399979

Table of Contents

Hand Jive

Count to 2 while tapping your right fist on top of your left fist.

Count to 2 while tapping your left fist on top of your right fist.

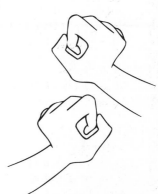

Count to 2 while clapping twice.

Combine all 3 movements, and repeat 3 times.

Body Jive

Count to 3 while stomping your foot.

Count to 3 with your right hand over your left, palms down, crossing them in a "scissors" fashion.

Count to 3 with your left hand over your right, palms down, crossing them in a "scissors" fashion.

Count to 3 while tapping your knees.

Combine all 4 movements, and repeat 3 times.

3

More Body Jive Counting

Count to 4 while tapping on your knee.

Count to 4 while clapping your hands.

Count to 4 while patting your chest.

Combine all of the movements while counting to 4, and repeat 3 times.

Create 4 movements of your own while counting to 4, and then combine them.

Music Fact

The Egyptian trumpet, found in a drawing in King Tut's tomb in Egypt, dates back over three thousand years. It is the oldest brass instrument we know about. This trumpet was a straightened tube about 4 feet long and was usually made from silver or bronze.

Music is counted by **beats**. Put your hand over your heart. Count 4 beats. Touch each heart below with your finger while you count to 4. Try tapping a row quickly or slowly. Each finger tap would be 1 beat.

Musical **beats** are combined in different patterns of 2's or 3's or 4's.

Which pattern shows beats in sets of 2?
Which pattern shows beats in sets of 3?
Which pattern shows beats in sets of 4?
Write the numbers 1-2, 1-2-3, or 1-2-3-4 under the black rectangles.

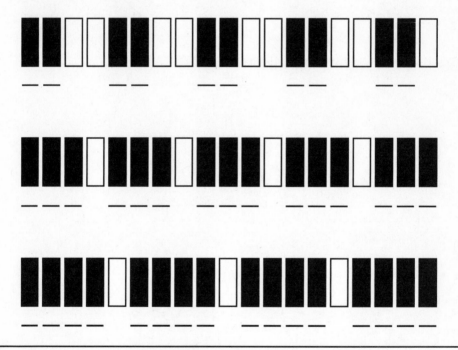

Music Fact

The humpback whale's call is the loudest noise made by a living creature. It can be heard from 500 miles away.

Create some patterns of your own.

Color the hearts in sets of 2.

Color the rectangles in sets of 3.

Some Are Weak, and Some Are Strong

Some beats are **weak**, and others are **strong**. Follow the ducks' beaks. The open beaks stand for strong beats. The closed beaks stand for weak beats. Tap the open beaks hard, and tap the closed beaks softly.

Some Are Strong, and Some Are Weak

Some beats are **weak**, and others are **strong**. Follow the ducks' beaks. The open beaks stand for strong beats. The closed beaks stand for weak beats. Tap the open beaks hard, and tap the closed beaks softly.

Musical beats are written as **notes**. Each musical note has a **head,** and most have a **stem**. When there is more than one note, the notes may be connected together with a **beam**.

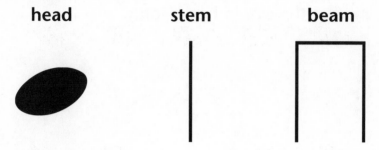

head   **stem**   **beam**

Draw a line to connect the note part to its name.

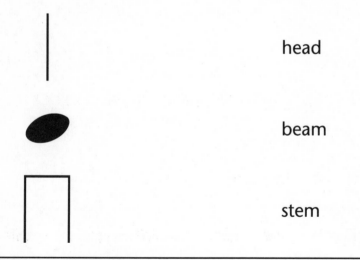

head

beam

stem

Music Fact
Violins are made up of over seventy separate pieces of wood.

Draw stems on the note heads.

Draw beams to join each pair of notes together.

© Rainbow Bridge Publishing

Introduction to Music—RB-904007

Music is made from notes that are in patterns. Find the patterns that are the **same** as this pattern (♩♩♩) and circle them in blue.

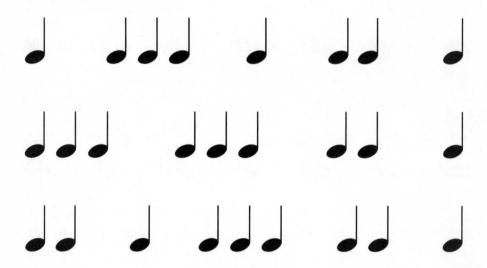

Find all of the music patterns that are **different** from this pattern (♩♩♩) and circle them in red.

www.summerbridgeactivities.com

Circle the notes that match this pattern (♩♩♩) in blue.
Circle the patterns that are different in red.

Find the notes that match this pattern (♩♩♩♩) and underline them in green.

    Introduction to Music—RB-904007

Think of all the different types of sounds you hear. There are long sounds and short sounds. Draw circles around the pictures of things that are short on this page. Draw squares around the pictures of things that are long.

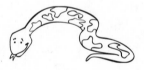
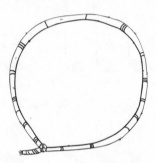

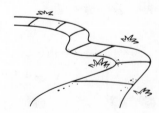

Think about sounds that you hear. Some of them last a long time, like a siren. Some of them last a short time, like a clap or a snap. Musical notes represent long and short sounds, too.

This is a **quarter note** ♩. It sounds like someone walking. Tap each note and say "walk."

walk   walk   walk   walk

This is an **eighth note** ♪. It stands for a shorter sound, like someone jogging. Tap each eighth note and say "jog."

jog   jog   jog   jog   jog   jog

Some notes last even longer, like walking slowly.

Some notes are even shorter, like running very quickly.

15

Write **walk** under the quarter notes and **jog** under the eighth notes.

Draw the correct note over the word.

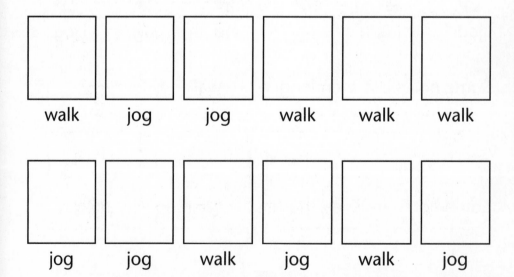

walk	jog	jog	walk	walk	walk

jog	jog	walk	jog	walk	jog

Cut out the boxes with notes and create your own patterns.

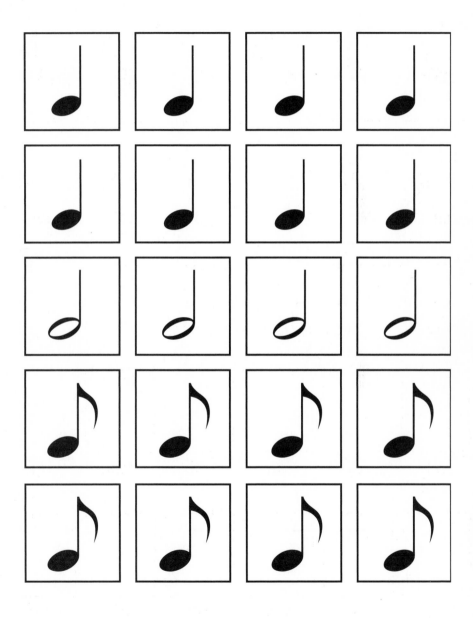

Introduction to Music—RB-904007

This page intentionally left blank to accommodate cutting activity on the opposite side.

Beats can be grouped together to make patterns. We call these patterns **rhythms**. We combine these different patterns together to make music.

We can find rhythms in things that surround us—even in the names of foods we eat! Tap each fruit while you say its name. Give one tap for each of its syllables. Tap once for *pear*. Tap twice, more quickly, for *apple*. Make three quicker taps for *strawberry* and four for *watermelon*.

Introduction to Music—RB-904007

The fruits are arranged in different orders. Tap the fruit and say the rhythm. Then draw the notes above the fruit:

♩ for pear, ♫ for apple, 𝅘𝅥𝅘𝅥𝅘𝅥 for strawberry, 𝅘𝅥𝅮𝅘𝅥𝅮𝅘𝅥𝅮𝅘𝅥𝅮 for watermelon

Draw the correct fruit under the note pattern.

Draw pictures of other fruits you can think of, and write their rhythms from the syllables.

Example:

orange

High Sounds

Think of all the different types of sounds you hear. There are high and low sounds. There are loud and soft sounds. Music is made up of all of these types of sounds.

Draw pictures of things that make high sounds.

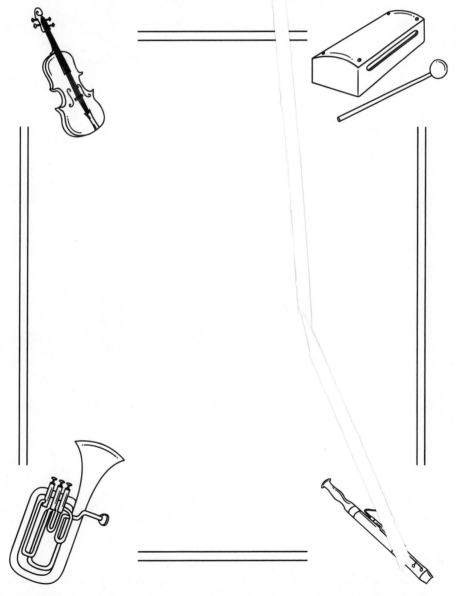

Introduction to Music—RB-904007

Low Sounds

In music, we say that high sounds and low sounds have a different **pitch**. Things that make a low sound have a low pitch.

Draw pictures of things that make **low** sounds.

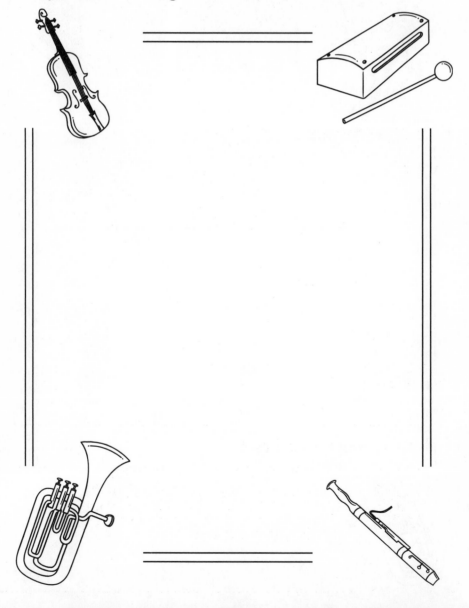

© Rainbow Bridge Publishing

Circle all of the pictures that make high sounds.
Underline all of the pictures that make low sounds.

Music Fact

Do you know what you really hear when you hold a seashell to your ear? It's not the sea—it's the echo of your blood pulsing in your ear.

Circle the end of the teeter-totter that is the highest with the color orange. Circle the end of the teeter-totter that is the lowest with the color blue.

Cut out the buttons on this page.

Introduction to Music—RB-904007

This page intentionally left blank to accommodate
cutting activity on the opposite side.

Place the buttons from page 27 that you cut out on the dots that are the highest on the page.

© Rainbow Bridge Publishing

Place the buttons from page 27 that you cut out on all of the dots that are the lowest on the page.

The **xylophone** is a musical instrument. It makes both low and high **pitches**. The smallest part of the xylophone makes the highest pitches. Color the 4 highest pitches red.

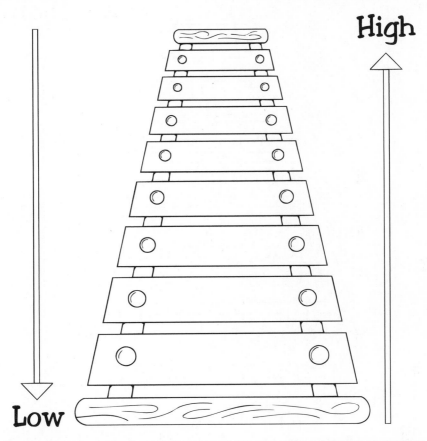

High

Low

Music Fact

Some male songbirds sing more than 2,000 times every day.

Introduction to Music—RB-904007

The widest part of the xylophone makes the lowest **pitches**. Color the 4 lowest pitches blue.

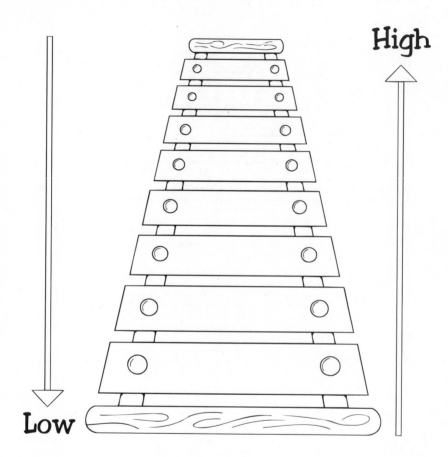

High

Low

Music Fact

Though many animals make noise with their throats, others don't. For example, a cricket's chirp is created when it rubs its wings together. Cicadas create sound by moving flaps of skin on their abdomens in and out.

www.summerbridgeactivities.com

Music patterns go up and down, like pitches go higher and lower. Some patterns go up. Help the bird get up to her nest by tracing the patterns of 3 up to her nest.

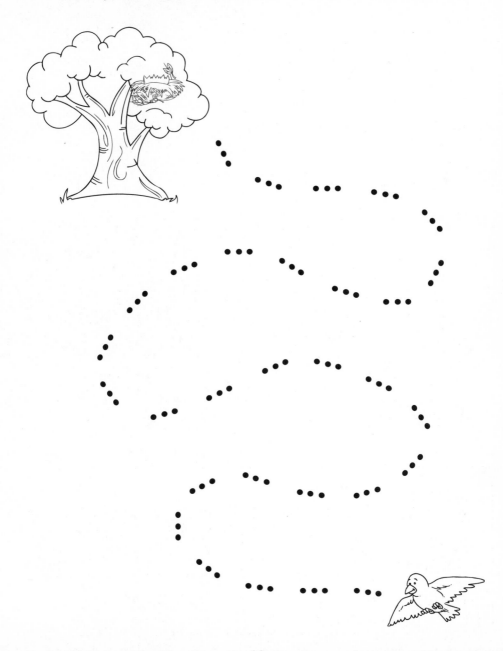

Some music patterns go down. Help the groundhog get to his home by tracing the patterns of 3 going down.

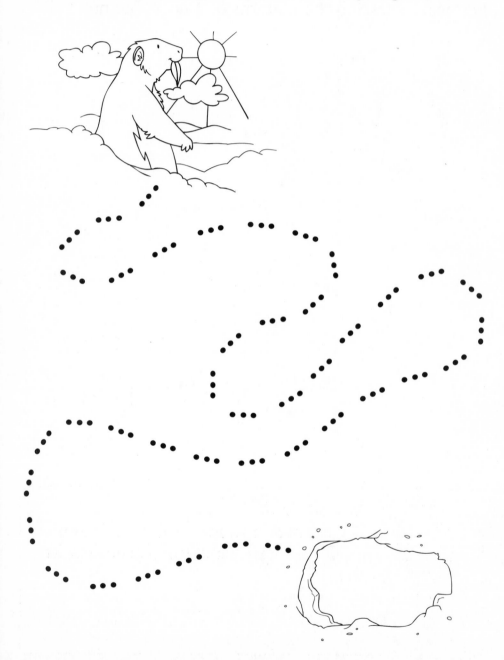

Some music patterns stay the same. Follow the duck floating on top of the water by tracing the patterns of 3.

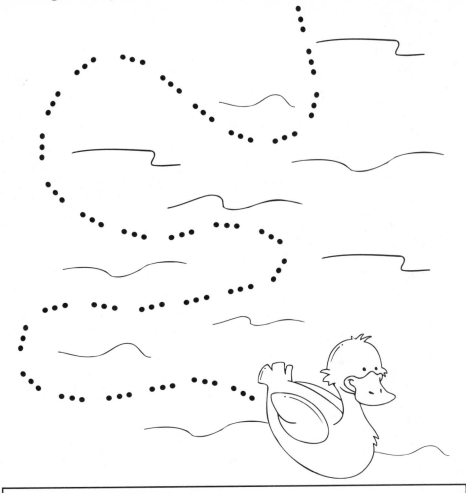

Music Fact

The *ocarina*, a wind instrument, is also called the "sweet potato" because of its shape.

Introduction to Music—RB-904007

Some music patterns combine up, down, and the same.
Circle all the groups of 4. Then label each group: U = up;
D = down; S = same.

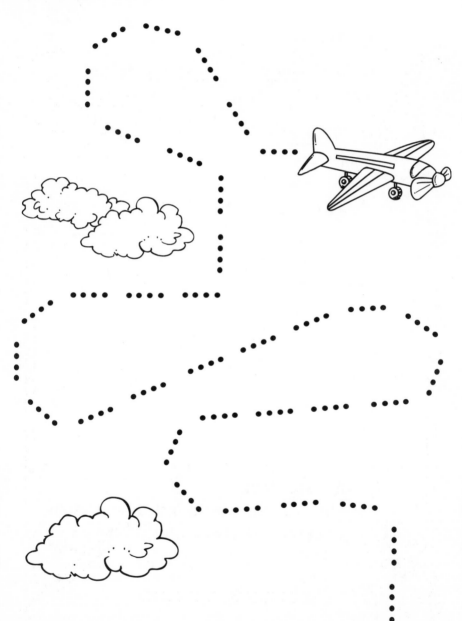

Create your own music patterns using up, down, and the same.

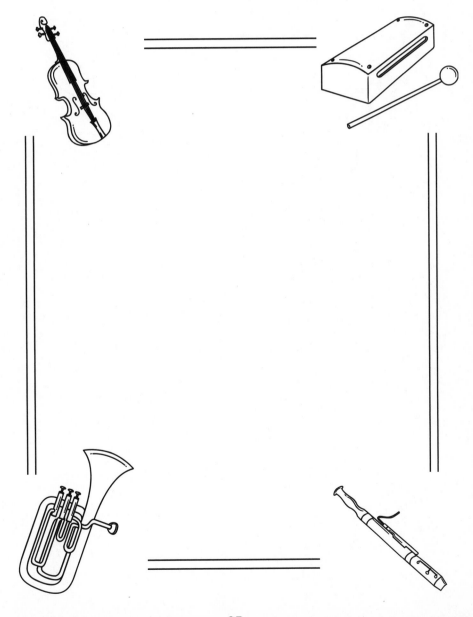

Introduction to Music—RB-904007

Loud and Soft

Take a sound walk and listen for sounds that you hear that are loud and soft. Draw pictures of things that you heard that made **loud** sounds.

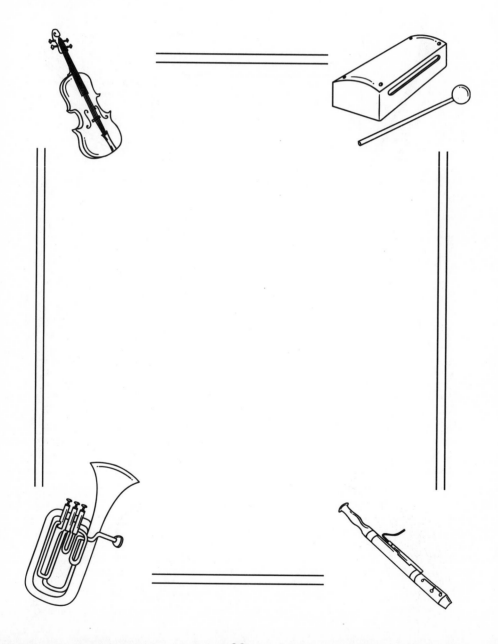

© Rainbow Bridge Publishing

Soft and Loud

Take a sound walk and listen for sounds you hear that are loud and soft. Draw pictures of things that you heard that made **soft** sounds.

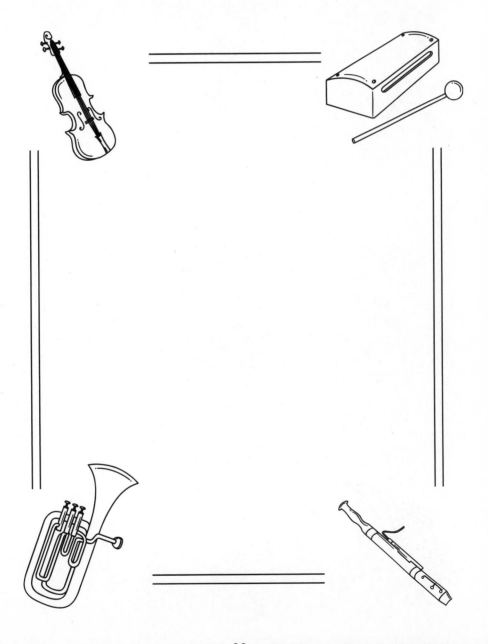

Introduction to Music—RB-904007

Circle the animals that make the **loudest** sounds in red.

Draw a blue box around the animals that make the **softest** sounds.

Introduction to Music—RB-904007

The music symbol for **soft** is *p*.
Practice writing the music symbol for soft.

_____

The music symbol for **loud** is *f*.
Practice writing the music symbol for loud.

_____

Music Fact

In the fifteenth century, a surgeon named Guido Lanfranc discovered that it is possible to check for skull fractures by putting a violin string between someone's teeth and plucking it. If the string makes a sweet note, the patient's head is fine. If the sound is muffled and dull, the patient has a fracture.

Music is written on a **staff**. A staff has 5 **lines**.

5 _____

4 _____

3 _____

2 _____

1 _____

Draw an X on the first line of the staff.

Draw an O on the second line of the staff.

Draw an X on the third line of the staff.

Draw an O on the fourth line of the staff.

Draw an X on the fifth line of the staff.

Music Fact
Can you guess what the world's best-selling musical instrument is?

_____ It's the harmonica!

A staff has 4 **spaces**.

4
3
2
1

Draw an O in the first space of the staff.

Draw an X in the second space of the staff.

Draw an O in the third space of the staff.

Draw an X in the fourth space of the staff.

Music Fact
Grand pianos can be played faster than upright pianos.

Some notes are written on the lines. The notes that are on lines are called **line notes**. Draw notes on the lines of the staff. Remember to include the heads and the stems.

Draw a circle around each of the line notes.

Music Fact

Telephones aren't just for talking! Music was sent down a telephone line the same year the phone was invented—1876.

www.summerbridgeactivities.com
© Rainbow Bridge Publishing

Some notes are written in the spaces. The notes that are in spaces are called **space notes**. Draw notes in the spaces of the staff. Remember to include the heads and the stems.

Draw a yellow square around each of the space notes.

Music Fact

Pianos are very impressive instruments. A piano can play notes lower than the lowest note of the double bassoon as well as notes higher than the top note of a piccolo.

Notes are placed on the staff to tell us if **pitches** are high or low. The high pitches are placed on the highest part of the staff. The lowest pitches are placed on the lowest part of the staff. Put an **H** below each high note. Put an **L** below each low note.

The highest pitches are placed on the highest part of the staff. Circle the highest notes on the staff in green.

The lowest pitches are placed on the lowest part of the staff. Draw a yellow square around the lowest notes on the staff.

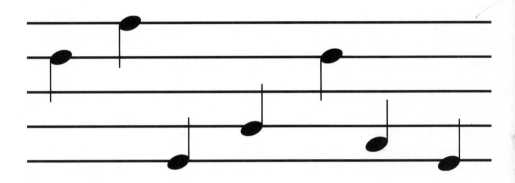

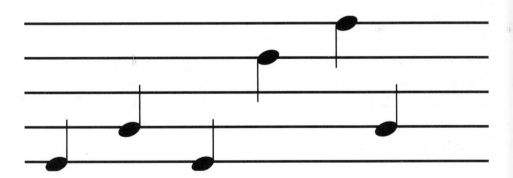

Introduction to Music—RB-904007

Draw notes on the highest lines.

Draw notes on the lowest lines.

Draw notes in the highest spaces.

Draw notes in the lowest spaces.

Introduction to Music—RB-904007

The Musical Alphabet

The notes on the lines and spaces create the pitches for music. The lines and spaces stand for pitches, or notes, in the musical alphabet. The **musical alphabet** has 7 notes: A-B-C-D-E-F-G. When you get to G, the alphabet starts over again.

Write the musical alphabet.

____   ____   ____   ____   ____   ____   ____

Write the notes that come next in the musical alphabet.

E   F   G

A   B   __

D   E   __

F   G   __   __

C   D   __   __   __

B   __   __   __

G   A   B   __   __

www.summerbridgeactivities.com

Write the missing letter from the musical alphabet on the blank line.

A   __   C   D

E   F   G   __

B   C   __   E

C   D   E   __

__   G   A   B

F   G   __   __   C

Music Fact

Different creatures can hear different sounds. Humans can hear sound waves with frequencies between 20 and 20,000 Hz. Dogs, on the other hand, can hear sounds between 50 and 45,000 Hz. Elephants can hear low sounds down to 5 Hz.

     Introduction to Music—RB-904007

Musical Pictures

Think of something that starts with each note of the musical alphabet and draw a picture of it.

A

B

C

D

Think of something that starts with each note of the musical alphabet and draw a picture of it.

E

F

G

Music Fact

Paul McCartney, one of the Beatles, recorded an ultrasonic whistle at the end of one of the group's songs. The whistle was too high for humans to hear. He recorded it for his dog to listen to.

Draw a line to connect the letter from the musical alphabet with the word that starts with that letter.

A   clarinet

B   gong

C   applause

D   flute

E   Bach

F   electric

G   drum

Music is created by putting different **rhythms** and **sounds** together. The sounds are made by **instruments**. Each instrument has a different sound. The materials that instruments are made of or the way they produce sounds determine the family that they belong to. Musical instruments are divided into four families. These families are called the **Woodwind Family**, the **Brass Family**, the **String Family**, and the **Percussion Family**.

Introduction to Music—RB-904007

The Woodwind Family gets its name because each of the instruments in the family either was originally made of wood or produces its sound by air blown across a wooden reed.

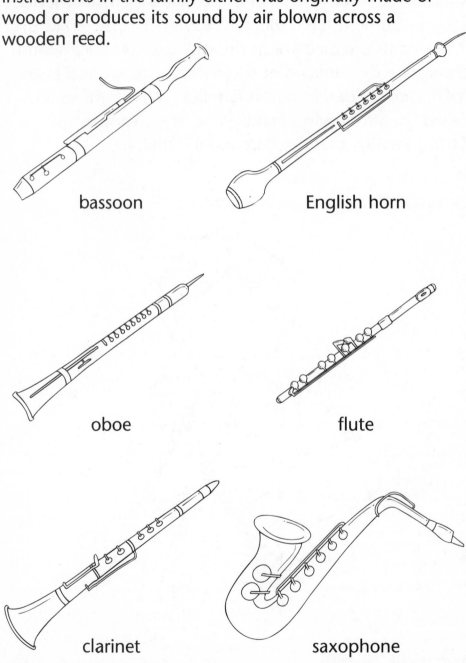

bassoon

English horn

oboe

flute

clarinet

saxophone

www.summerbridgeactivities.com

© Rainbow Bridge Publishing

Connect the dots and name the woodwind instrument.

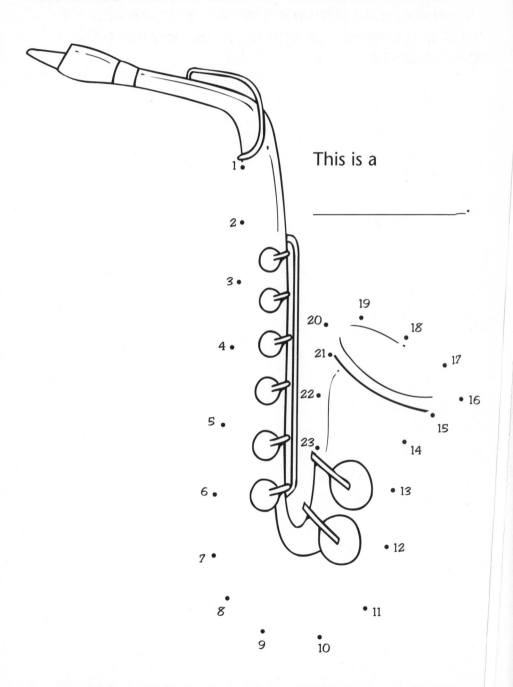

This is a

_____.

Introduction to Music—RB-904007

Which instrument is missing from the Woodwind Family?
Draw the missing instrument. Write the name of each
instrument below its picture: **bassoon, English horn,
oboe, saxophone, clarinet, flute.**

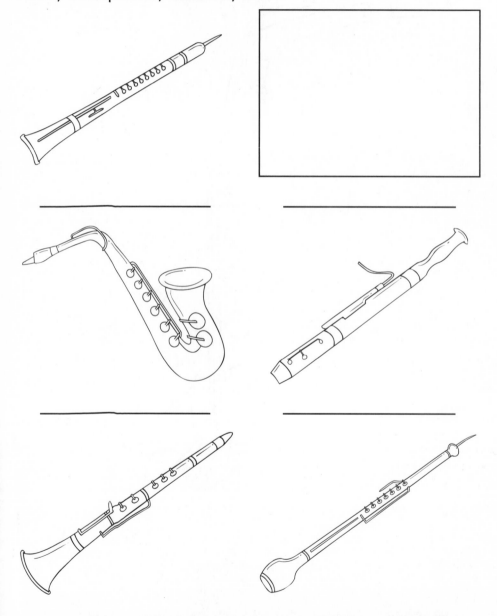

Woodwind Match

Draw a line to connect the instrument's picture to its name.

clarinet

bassoon

flute

English horn

saxophone

oboe

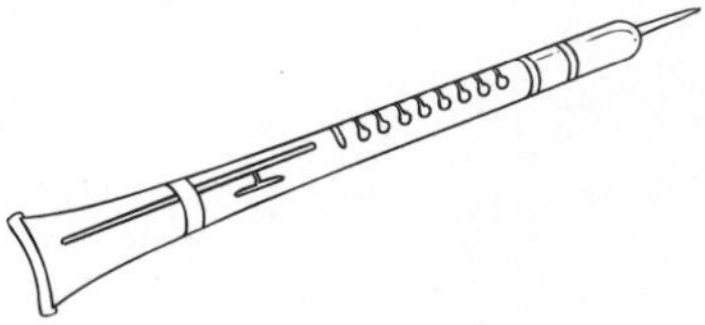

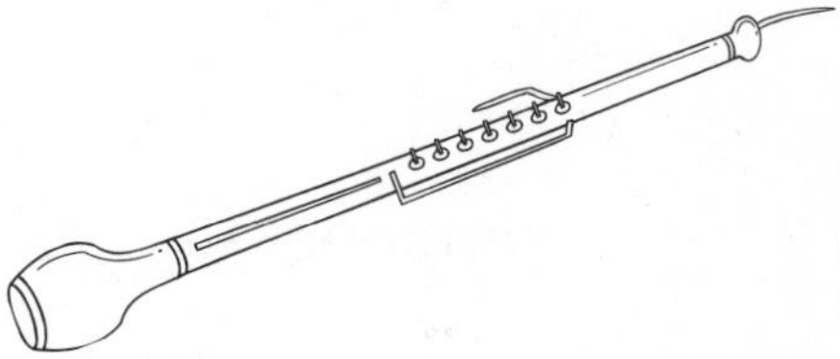

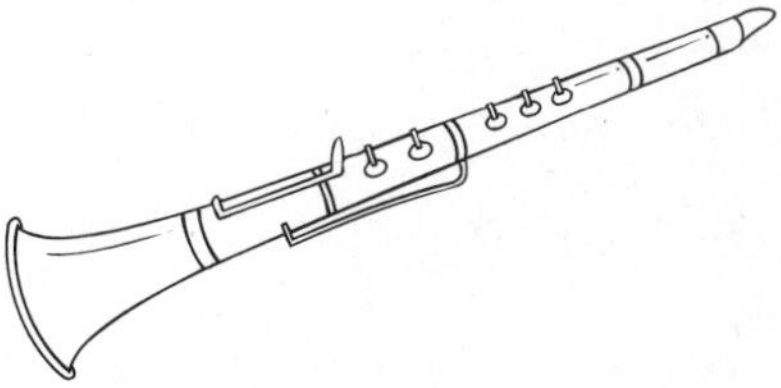

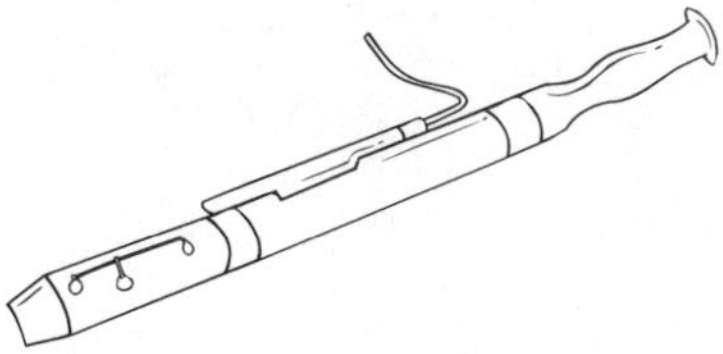

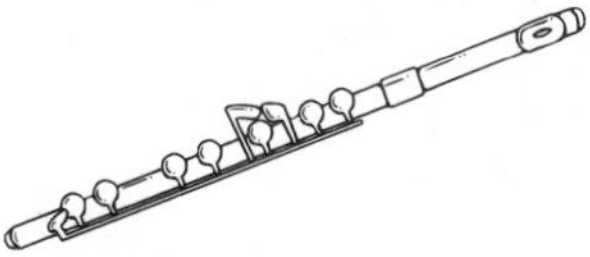

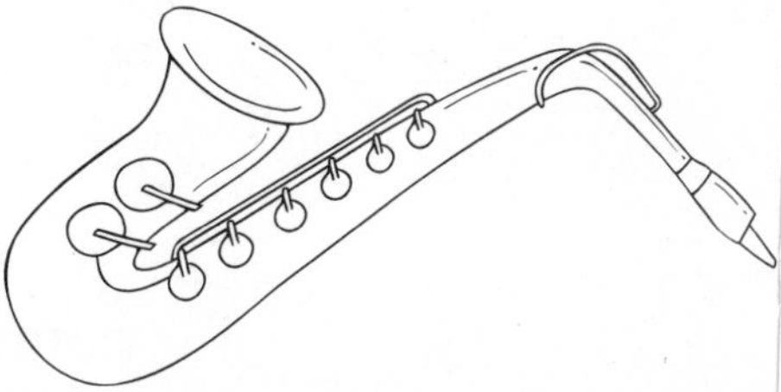

The Brass Family gets its name because each of the instruments in the family is made from the metal brass.

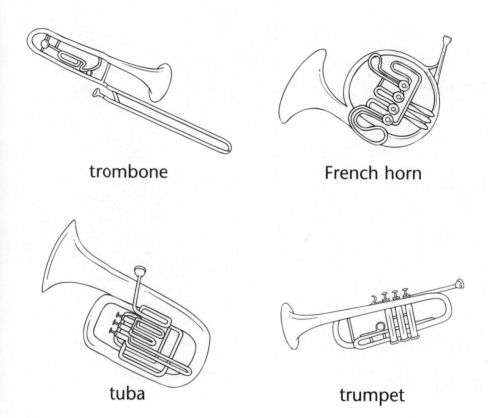

trombone

French horn

tuba

trumpet

baritone

Connect the dots and name the brass instrument.

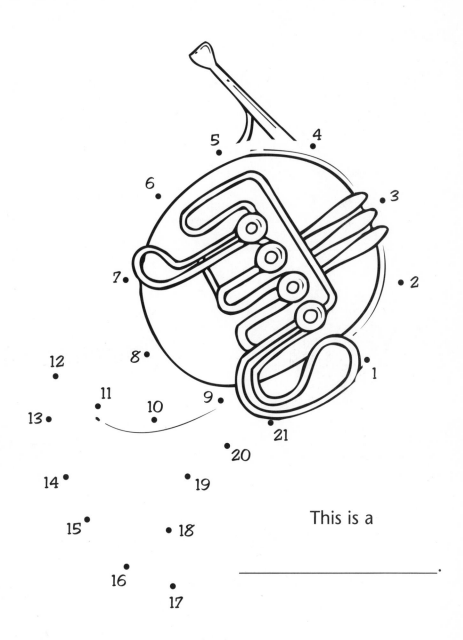

This is a

_____.

Which instrument is missing from the Brass Family? Draw the missing instrument. Write the name of each instrument below its picture: **trumpet, trombone, tuba, baritone, French horn**.

_____

_____

_____

_____

_____

Draw a line to connect the instrument's picture to its name.

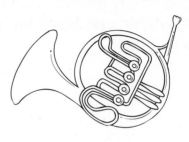

trumpet

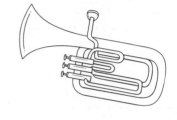

tuba

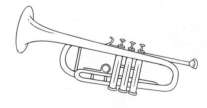

trombone

French horn

baritone

The String Family

The String Family gets its name because each instrument in the family has strings that produce sound when struck, plucked, or played with a bow.

double bass

cello

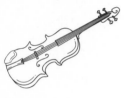

viola

violin

harp

piano

guitar

banjo

www.summerbridgeactivities.com   © Rainbow Bridge Publishing

String Dot-to-Dot

Connect the dots and name the string instrument.

This is a

_____.

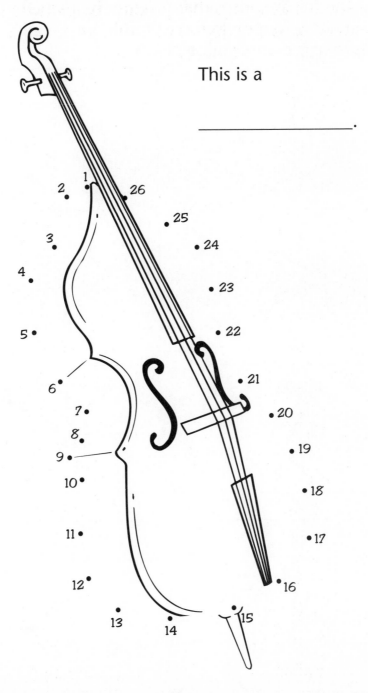

Which instrument is missing from the String Family?
Draw the missing instrument. Write the name of each
instrument below its picture: **double bass, cello, viola,
violin, harp, piano, guitar, banjo**.

_____

_____

_____

_____

_____

_____

_____

Draw a line to connect the instrument's picture to its name.

piano

guitar

banjo

double bass

cello

viola

harp

violin

© Rainbow Bridge Publishing

Introduction to Music—RB-904007

The Percussion Family

The Percussion Family gets its name because each instrument in the family is struck or shaken in order to make a sound. (*Percuss* means "to tap.")

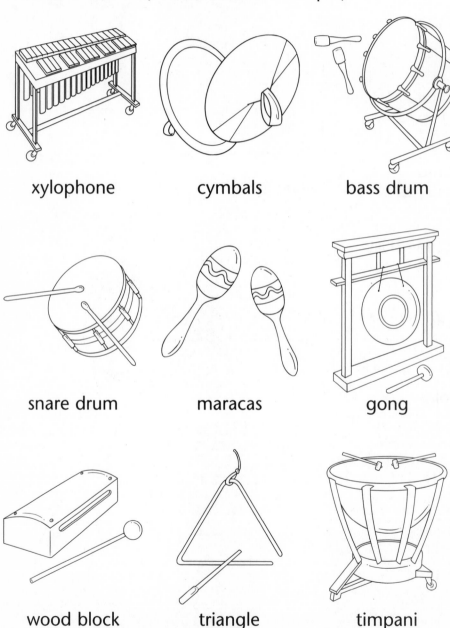

xylophone   cymbals   bass drum

snare drum   maracas   gong

wood block   triangle   timpani

Connect the dots and name the percussion instrument.

These are

_____.

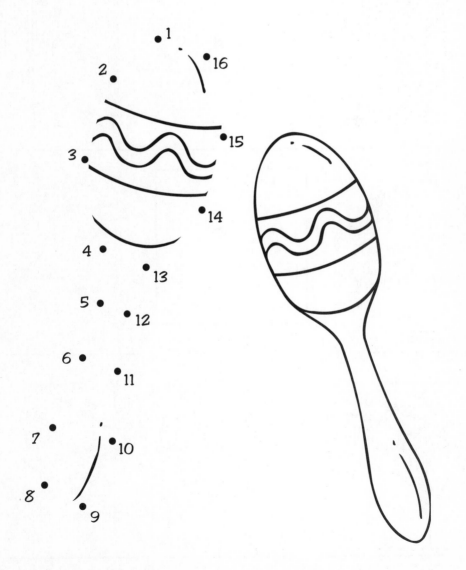

© Rainbow Bridge Publishing

Introduction to Music—RB-904007

Which instrument is missing from the Percussion Family? Draw the missing instrument. Write the name of each instrument below its picture: **bass drum, cymbals, triangle, xylophone, snare drum, timpani, gong, wood block, maracas.**

_____

_____

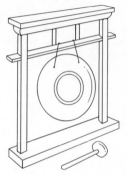

_____

_____

_____

_____

_____

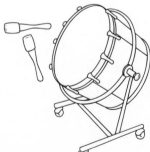

_____

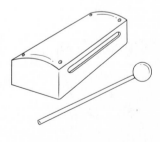

_____

Percussion Match

Draw a line to connect the instrument's picture to its name.

bass drum

gong

triangle

xylophone

wood block

cymbals

timpani

snare drum

maracas

© Rainbow Bridge Publishing   Introduction to Music—RB-904007

Answer Pages

Page 6

Page 13

(□ = circled in red)

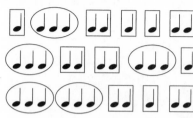

Page 10

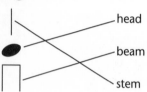

Page 12

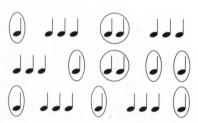

Page 16

www.summerbridgeactivities.com

© Rainbow Bridge Publishing

Answer Pages

Page 20

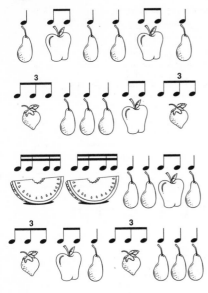

Page 21

Page 26

Page 31

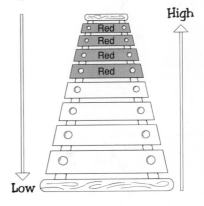

Page 32

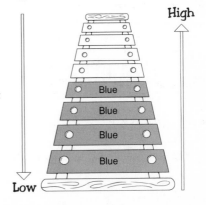

Answer Pages

Page 43

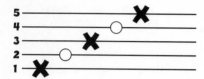

Page 44

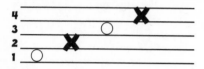

Page 46

Page 48

Page 49

L L H L H H H

H L L L H H H

Page 50

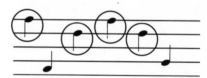

Page 51

Page 54
A B C D E F G
E F <u>G</u>
A B <u>C</u>
D E <u>F</u>
F G <u>A</u> <u>B</u>
C D <u>E</u> <u>F</u> <u>G</u>
B <u>C</u> <u>D</u> E <u>F</u>
G A B <u>C</u> <u>D</u>

Page 55
A <u>B</u> C D
E F G <u>A</u>
B C <u>D</u> E
C D E <u>F</u>
<u>F</u> G A B
F G <u>A</u> <u>B</u> C

Page 58

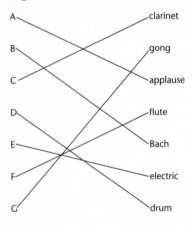

Page 61
saxophone

Page 62
The flute is missing.

Page 63

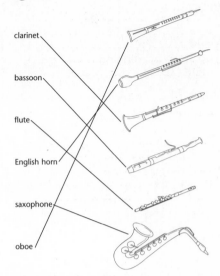

Page 65
French horn

Page 66
The trumpet is missing.

Page 67

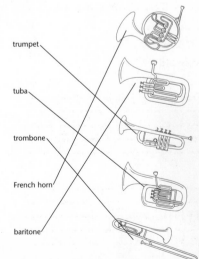

79

Answer Pages

Page 69
double bass

Page 70
The harp is missing.

Page 71

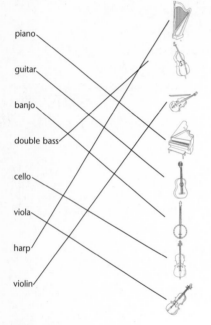

Page 73
maracas

Page 74
The cymbals are missing.

Page 75

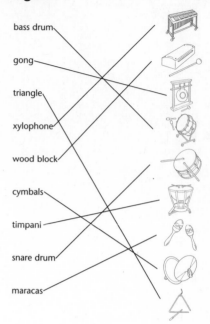